My F

The Deaconess Role

From A Biblical Perspective

Dr. Joseph R. Rogers, Sr.

Copyright:

This is the sole material of Joseph R. Rogers, Sr. and it is not to be copied or sold without written consent.

(cc: 2011)

Dedication

Again, the Lord has favoured me to share with you another book. This time it is about the church **"Deaconess",** a role that has been debated over the years as to how this office came into being and its function in the church. There may be a few views; I hold only two: the **traditional, (denominational) or conventional (biblical).**

I will expound further, whether or not the **"Deaconess"** is a wife of a **"Deacon"** or **an ordained female servant.** There are different views surrounding the subject but I would like to share this writing from a biblical perspective.

In doing so, I would like to dedicate this writing to all **'deaconess'** and/or **'deacons'**-female who have given of themselves to ministering to/in the local church.

It is my payer that this material will help you in your ministry and shed some light, as it relates to your function or in the body of Christ and your local church.

In closing, I do not declare to be an authority on this subject matter; therefore I lean only on the divine scriptures for knowledge and insight.

God Bless,

Dr. Joseph R. Rogers, Sr.

Table Of Contents

	Page No.
Dedication	3
Introduction	7
I. Chapter One	11
(The Origin Of Deaconess)	
II. Chapter Two	22
(Who Is A Deaconess?)	
A. The Traditional View	
B. The Biblical View	
III. Chapter Three	30
(Biblical Example of Deaconess)	
IV. Chapter Four	35
(The Importance of Deaconess)	
V. Chapter Five	45
(How To Select Deaconess)	

                                    Page No.

VI. Conclusion---------------------   50

   (Overview of Deaconess)

VII. For Your Consideration----------   54

VIII. Author's Contact/Other Works---   73

IX. Notes --------------------------   85

Introduction

According to the book of I Timothy Chapter 3, all that is expected of a deacon (or deaconess) and their wives (spouses) is explicit, straight forward, open and direct.

In Verse 11 of that same chapter it clearly states what is expected of the deaconess – Deaconess: they must be sober-minded women, not slanderers, but in every way temperate and trustworthy (Weymouth New Testament).

From this we can/need to understand what the bible says about the office or ministry of the deacon(ess)

There two schools of thought as to who a deaconess is:

1. The Traditional School of thought identifies a **'deaconess'** as the wife of deacon (male) while,

2. The Conventional School of thought regards a **'deaconess'** as an ordained female who has had hands laid on them just as the male.

However, neither of these schools of thought is **irrelevant** – what is important is that a deaconess should to be grave, not a slanderer, sober, and faithful in all things.

Therefore, the requirements of a deaconess office are synonymous to the requirements of the office of a bishop or pastor, regardless of whether she is the wife of a deacon or an ordained female servant.

In my personal opinion, I think it's more appropriate to consider both categories of deaconesses in the church; that is, to ordain female servants as deaconesses and also extend leadership responsibilities to the deacon's wife.

This book will capture the details of who deaconess are, what are their duties and the criteria surrounding their selection and more.

In a word of wisdom and caution, do not go to a church that does not ordain females as 'deacons' and try to force this issue. It is not worth the conversation or challenge.

You will cause more trouble than you will resolve. The Gospel validates all things: allow the Holy Spirit to resolve the situation.

The key to understanding this issue is to know what the bible says and apply those principles. Never follow everyone's opinions and beliefs: follow the Lord.

Be Blessed,

Dr. Joseph R. Rogers, Sr.

I. CHAPTER ONE
(THE ORIGIN OF DEACONESS)

The word Deacon and/or Deaconess are English word and were derived from the Greek word **diaconos**, meaning a **servant**. It is important to note that the original Greek word was used in a general sense for all servants, i.e., **pastor, elder, apostle, prophet**...with no religious connotation.

However, when certain active church members were given the responsibility of handling practical matters in the church of God the apostles adopted the term for those individuals.

This began with **"The Seven"** (the number of completion) the original servants in **Acts 6:1-6, 21:8:**

"But as the believers rapidly multiplied, there were rumblings of discontent".

(1) The Greek-speaking believers complained about the Hebrew-speaking believers, saying that their widows were being discriminated against in the daily distribution of food.

(2) So the Twelve (Apostles) called a meeting of all the believers. They said, "We apostles should spend our time teaching the word of God, not running a food program.

(3) And so, brothers, **select** (choose, decide on) seven men who are well respected and are full of the Spirit (Holy Ghost) and **wisdom** (insight, knowledge, understanding). We will **give them** this responsibility.

(4) Then we apostles can spend our time in prayer and teaching the word.

(5) Everyone liked this idea, and they chose the following: **Stephen** (a man full of faith and the Holy Spirit), **Philip, Procorus, Nicanor, Timon, Parmenas,** and **Nicolas** of Antioch (an earlier convert to the Jewish faith).

(6) These seven were **presented** (offered) to the apostles, who **prayed** for them as they **laid their hands on them.**"

Acts 21:8-"The next day we went on to Caesarea and stayed at the home of **Philip, the Evangelist,** one of the seven men who had been chosen to distribute food."

These seven were regarded as an element of the "ministry" - minister/servant/deacon, all, originated from the same Greek word i.e., deacons primarily served **(diakonein)** the physical needs of people so that the apostles could concentrate on ministering **(diakonia)** the Word of God.

Deacons were not however limited, some of the deacons were also **teachers and evangelists**, as was **Stephen** who is often regarded as the first Christian martyr (Acts 7:1-60), and **Philip** who successfully preached in Samaria (Acts 8:5-13) and baptized one of the first converts from Africa, the Ethiopian eunuch (Acts 8:26-38).

The roots of Deaconesses can be traced from the time of Jesus Christ through the 13th century. Evidence for the presence of ordained female deacons in the early Christian period is "clear and unambiguous" according to the Bible.

Deaconesses existed from the early Byzantine periods in Constantinople and Jerusalem; although the office may not have been in existence throughout the European churches.

The female diaconate in the Byzantine Church and middle Byzantine periods were recognized as one of the major orders of clergy. A modern resurgence of the office began in the early nineteenth century in both Europe and North America.

Presently, Deaconesses are present in many countries of the world, except in the Roman Catholic Church, in which it is hols that ordained ministry is restricted to men.

According to the book of I Timothy 3:8-13, it is not certain whether a wife of a deacon is automatically a deaconess or not because the qualifications were equally applied.

I Timothy 3:8-13 (AKJV):

"Likewise must the deacons be grave, not double-tongued, not given too much wine, not greedy of filthy lucre; holding the mystery of the faith in a pure conscience. And let these also first be proved; then let them use the office of a deacon, being found blameless. **Even so must their wives** be grave, not slanderers, sober and faithful in all things. Let the deacon be the husband of one wife, ruling their children and their own houses well. For they that have used the office of a deacon well purchase to themselves a good degree, and great boldness in the faith which is in Christ Jesus."

From this text one can draw a few views as to its meaning:

1. Is the **deacon** to be the same as Bishop or pastor of the congregation? Well, it is clear that the 'deacon' and bishop or pastor is not the same function or calling. The deacons are **selected and**

appointed, the pastor or bishop are **called and anointed** by God.

2. Is the **deacon's wife** automatically a deaconess because she is the wife of a deacon (male)? Well, the text does not say that, but traditionally this view has been accepted. I hold the biblical view that the **'deaconess'** is an **ordained female** that operates in the deacon's ministry of the church.

I know that there will be a difference of opinions on this subject, but let us not **separate** ourselves because of it. You must agree that the end results of this office is **doing ministry.**

Again, what does 'likewise' mean? Does it mean likewise as servants of God? It is known from the writings of early church history that deaconesses served prominently by caring for needy fellow believers, visiting the sick, and assisting in the baptism of female converts. **Phoebe** is perhaps the best-known deaconess in the Bible record.

"I commend to you our sister **Phoebe, a servant (deaconess)** of the **church at Cenchreae,** that you may receive her in the Lord as befits the saints, and help her in whatever she may require from you, for she has been a helper of many and of myself as well" **(Romans 16:1-2 RSV)**

"Therefore, my brethren, whom I love and long for, my joy and crown, stand firm thus in the Lord, my beloved. I entreat Euodia and I entreat Syntyche to agree in the Lord. And I ask you also, true yokefellow, help these women, for they have labored (servants) side by side with me in the gospel together with Clement and the rest of my fellow workers, whose names are in the book of life." **(Philippians 4:1-3 RSV)**

II. CHAPTER TWO
(WHO IS A DEACONESS)

As earlier mentioned before, there are two views as to who a deaconess is: the first view regards a deaconess as the wife of a deacon while the second regards her as an ordained female servant.

In either case, the core values of a deaconess are not different from a deacon. In this Chapter we shall consider both concerns **vis-à-vis** from biblical and practical perspectives.

A. DEACONESS - <u>TRADITIONAL VIEW</u>

With reference to our text in the book of I Timothy 3:8-13, understanding the character of a Deaconess should be clear.

The concept of marriage as an oath that binds a man and a woman as a single entity before God can also be used to justify the **automatic qualification** of the wife of a deacon as a deaconess – **Genesis 2:24** "Therefore shall a man leave his father and his mother, and shall cleave unto his wife: and they shall be one flesh".

Traditionally, the Deaconess is the wife of a husband who is a Deacon. Let me be clear that my aim is not to confuse this situation, but to bring some biblical clarity that should help us understand this frequently debated topic. **Traditionally** the deaconess will assist the deacons in the following areas:

1. Assists her husband in home and hospital visits.
2. Assists the Deacons in carrying out Baptism and the Lord's Supper.
3. Assists in spiritual counseling to females of the church.
4. Assists in giving instructions to single women, wives and young teens in church. Also etiquette, church protocol and general matters of faith are covered.
5. Other duties as deemed fit by the leadership of the local church.

6. Assists in giving godly instructions in holiness, character and integrity.

The deaconess depending upon how she carries herself in character and integrity can either help her husband or minimize his effectiveness with sinful actions.

B. DEACONESS - BIBLICAL VIEW

The Bible views Deacon as ordained servant and therefore, expects them (him or her) to have the following attributes:

1. Be grave,

2. Not double-tongued,

3. Not given to much wine,

4. Not greedy of filthy lucre,

5. Holding the mystery of the faith in a pure conscience,

6. And let these also first be proved; then let them use the office of a deacon, being found blameless,

Sometimes we look for a lot of material on a subject matter, but I learned to trust and follow the bible for true directions. When we follow the scriptures, I know it will direct down the path of **rightness** and **righteousness**.

Deacon(ness) are selected to assist the pastors in carrying out the **functions, plans, destinies or vision** of the local church—do that with joy!

Again, the interpretation of this verse, I Timothy 3:11 are two-folds:

   a. **Deaconess** is a **ordained women** or
   b. **Deaconess** is the **wife of a deacon.**

In either case, as Christians, the bible expects us to focus on the **attributes and duties** of the office and not the personalities in the office.

What should matter most in this office are the **character, integrity, transparency** and **behaviour** of the Deacon/Deaconess regardless as to whether **she** is the wife of an ordained Deacon or **she herself** is an ordained servant.

Therefore, it is normal if this verse of the Bible **(I Timothy 3:11)** is **interpreted** as automatically conferring the powers and duties of a Deacon on the **wife of a deacon** – regardless, she must **behave just like her husband.**

Again, as mentioned earlier, if the Bible sees a husband and his wife as one, then one can say **logically** and **interpret** I Timothy 3:11 as an automatic qualification of a wife of a **Deacon** as a Deaconess.

However, it will be more appropriate if she (the wife) is ordained (hands laid on) as her husband.

In light of this situation, is the wife of a **'pastor' a pastor (ness),** the wife of a **'prophet' a prophet (ess),** the wife or an **'apostle' an apostle (ness),** the wife of an **'evangelist'** an **'evangelist (nes)?**

Not necessarily so, this is why I believe that just as the local church is able to ordain a **man**, so is they should be able to ordain a **woman**.

III. CHAPTER THREE
(BIBLICAL EXAMPLE OF A DEACONESS)

In the servant ministry, the **role** of the female should not be different from the role of the male as long as both sexes have been **anointed** to occupy their respective offices.

The only exception is when it comes to dealing with the opposite sexes. Both men and women must be extremely careful in this area.

We're all human and it does not matter how anointed we are, how knowledgeable we claim to be, how much experience we claim to have-**the devil will always tempt us.**

We have been given authority to deal with evil, but more so, it is our responsibility to do ministry in the church. Let us remember that God is our source! Consider Romans 16:1, 2 where Paul speaks of **Phoebe as a servant of the church.** This is clearly a diaconal role - the Bible is not talking of having authority here, but the service factor.

In a certain setting (local churches), hot debates among some ministers have arisen from this topic. "We need to biblical when we discuss the deacon's and/or deaconess' role.

I believe the Bible is the authority in ordaining women as deacons. Women have been used throughout church history (New & Old) Testament! Let us not **gauge** this issue from a **denominational, traditional or personal** perspective, but a **biblical one.**

Now, let us take a look at some Biblical examples of Deaconesses:

a. **Romans 16:1-4 (NLT)** "I commend to you our sister **Phoebe**, who is a deacon in the church in Cenchrea. Welcome her in the Lord as one who is worthy of honor among God's people. Help her in whatever she needs, for she has been helpful to many, and especially to me. Give my greetings to Priscilla and Aquila, my co-workers in the ministry of Christ Jesus. In fact, they once risked their lives for me. I am thankful to them, and so are all the Gentile churches."

b. **Acts 9:36 (NKJ)** "Now there was at Joppa a certain disciple named Tabitha, which by interpretation is called **Dorcas:** this woman was full of good works and almsdeeds which she did."

c. **St. Luke 8:3 (NLT)** "**Joanna**, the wife of Chuza, Herod's business manager; Susanna; and many others who were contributing from their own resources to support Jesus and his disciples."

All these women carried out their expected **Servant's duties.**

A deaconess is, therefore, expected to perform no less than each of the mentioned women.

In closing, God has used, is using and will continue to use **'women'** in the body of Christ and the local church setting.

IV. CHAPTER FOUR
(THE DEACONESS IMPORTANCE)

While the Bible does not explicitly institute the office of the deaconess, or use this title, there are many scriptures that helped form this vocation in the early church as congregations provided care for those in need.

In this chapter, we will examine some of those passages, and hopefully we will learn how the church can use the vocation of deaconess to help care both physically and spiritually of those in need.

THE DEACONESSES' ATTENTION:

The Deacons became known in the Bible when they were overwhelmed with having to ministers perform the physical needs of the church.

The Apostles' primary roles were: teaching and preaching the word of God. It is a wonderful thing to see the local church functioning as the Lord has directed: the pastor preaching and the deacons assist him/her, as they perform their appointed duties. I said, <u>"Their appointed duties";</u> **not duties they have misinterpreted having—that is, controlling the church!**

I must say as I have stated in my books, **"Church Leadership and My Role As**

A Deacon"; the deacon/deaconess were never selected, appointed and confirmed to **pastor the Pastor or pastor the church—they were called to assist!** See the following Bible passages:

Acts 6:1, 3 (NKJV) — "And in those days, when the number of the disciples was multiplied, there arose a murmuring of the Grecians against the Hebrews, because their widows were neglected in the daily ministration. [3] Wherefore, brethren, look ye out among you seven men of honest report, full of the Holy Ghost and wisdom, whom we may **appoint over this business**".

Ezekiel 34:4 – "The diseased have you not strengthened, neither have you healed that which was sick, neither have you bound up that which was broken, neither have you brought again that which was driven away, neither have you sought that which was lost; but with force and with cruelty have you ruled them."

St. Luke 7:2– "And a certain centurion's servant, who was dear unto him, was sick, and ready to die."

Each of these Bible passages describes a problem in areas where the Deaconess becomes **relevant in the church of God.**

Let's see a few passages that reveal how the needs of these individuals are to be met, as well as some ways by which Deaconesses can help meet the needs of these individuals as they work alongside the pastor:

I Timothy 5:16 (International Standard Version): "If any woman is a believer and has relatives who are widows, she should help them. The church should not be burdened, so it can help those widows who have no other family members to care for them."

James 1:27 (NKJV) – "Pure religion and undefiled before God and the Father is this, To visit the fatherless and widows in their affliction, and to keep himself unspotted from the world."

Romans 15:26 (American KJV): "For it has pleased them of Macedonia and Achaia to make a certain contribution for the poor saints which are at Jerusalem."

James 5:14 (Webster's Bible Translation): "Is any sick among you? let him call for the elders of the church; and let them pray over him, anointing him with oil in the name of the Lord:"

Romans 12:20 (International Standard Version): "But "if your enemy is hungry, feed him. For if he is thirsty, give him a drink. If you do this, you will pile burning coals on his head.""

Therefore, the office of the deaconess must reach out to those in need. God through Jesus Christ reached out and down to help humanity, so likewise must this office assist in the same manner.

Why should it be a concern of the church (deacon, deaconess) to care for people? Let us look at Matthew 9:12-13 and I Corinthians 12:12-26 for the answers to these questions.

St. Matthew 9:12-13 (American KJV): "But when Jesus heard that, he said to them, They that be whole need not a physician, but they that are sick. But go you and learn what that means, I will have mercy, and not sacrifice: for I am not come to call the righteous, but sinners to repentance."

I Corinthians 12:12-26, will also give us some insight as to what is expected of the church through this office.

We live in a sinful world full of broken people who are struggling not only physically and emotionally but also spiritually.

Deaconesses are trained to address physical needs through acts of mercy and provide spiritual care to those in need.

If you read the passages below, you should be able to **identify** the spiritual needs and the way a Deaconess could address these needs.

Whatever the case, a Deaconess needs to be ordained for this work because the job she is expected to do is enormous and can be overwhelming most of the time.

Jude 1:21 (NIV): "Keep yourselves in God's love as you wait for the mercy of our Lord Jesus Christ to bring you to eternal life. Be merciful to those who doubt;"

Also **Romans 6** and **Luke 5:17-26** mention some spiritual needs that can be carried out by the deaconess. Please note that the Deaconesses may serve in a variety of different positions (congregations, institutions or in the mission field).

It should be clear that the Deaconess Ministry is needed and is an important component in the body of Christ. For one to **minimize** this great ministry is to **not appreciate** what great blessings the Lord has for his church.

I **commend** those women who have been reaching out, who are reaching out and who will continue to reach out in the future.

V. CHAPTER FIVE
(HOW TO SELECT A DEACONESS)

The selection of a Deaconess should be under the leading of the Holy Spirit. Our earlier text, Acts 6:1-6, clearly demonstrates the normal selection criteria that should be adopted by any Bible believing Church.

In fact, no method of selecting Deaconesses should fall short of the one explained in this text. In this chapter, we shall be considering the elements of selecting a Deaconess.

Below are some **expected attributes of a Deaconess**; this means that whoever does not possess these attributes should not be considered for the office of Deaconess Ministry.

This sound **repetitive** but the deacon must be:

1. Be grave,
2. Not double-tongued,
3. Not given to much wine,
4. Not greedy of filthy lucre,
5. Holding the mystery of the faith in a pure conscience.
6. And let these also first be proved; then let them use the office of a deacon, being found blameless.

In verse 11 of I Timothy 3 it says "**their wives**" -

rather, "**the women,**" that is, **the Deaconesses.**

Conversely, this verse could be interpreted as **"if the wives of the deacons were meant, there seems no reason for the omission of "their" (not in the Greek)"**.

Also the Greek for "even so" (the same as for **"likewise,"** 1 Timothy 3:8, and **"in like manner,"** 1 Timothy 2:9), denotes a transition to another class of persons.

Further, there were doubtless Deaconesses at Ephesus, such as **Phoebe** was at Cenchrea (Ro. 16:1, **"servant,"**

Greek, "**deaconess**"), yet no mention is made of them in this Epistle.

The role of the Holy Spirit in the selection of a Deaconess is very important and we must never at anytime select anyone based upon our own thinking.

This office is **biblical** and it must be filled by those persons who know The Lord as Saviour and Lord. Remember, if a person knows not the Lord, he/she will not know how to minister in the Lord's Church (to the people).

Furthermore, I have discussed in two of my other writings, "**My Role As A Deacon** and **Church Leadership-The Pastor &**

The Deacon", that the deacon or pastor; as well as the **'deaconess'** should not be selected on the basis of:

        1. Popularity

        2. Beauty

        3. Civic Status or

        4. Political Status

Even though the above list have their places in life, the selecting of the **'deaconess'** or **"servant"** must be accomplished only by **biblical and spiritual insights and knowledge.**

VI. CONCLUSION

The meaning of **gunikos** in I Timothy 3:11 have been debated many times throughout the history of the church. Some conservative evangelical scholars have adopted a variety of possibilities, but the primary issue under consideration deals with the role of women within the church.

Based upon the referenced verses in this book, **I do believe** that **woman (female)** should serve as **servants (ministers)** in the church (I take into consideration the account of Deaconess Phoebe).

Nevertheless, depending upon which view you hold: a deaconess as an ordained woman or a deaconess as the wife of a deacon, the essence here is **'ministry'** and not **'title'** or **'name'**.

I, therefore, conclude the following based on the evidence, I accept both views - **the view which suggests these women were the wives of deacons,** as well that the view which says the women were ordained deaconesses, because both can qualify.

I do not believe the text is limiting feminine "deacon work" (i.e. areas of practical service) only to the deacon's wife, but rather assuming they will have some minor role due to their proximity with their husbands.

Additionally, I have no problem with a special set of women (in an office setting...related/not related personally to the deacons...under the authority of the Holy Spirit) who has the ability to minister to other women and needy people in the church (like those in the early church who visited the sick, distributed provisions among the poor, aided women in baptismal ceremonies, visited Christian women in pagan households, assisted the ill, comforted the lonely, visited those in jail and need prayer).

Without a doubt, there are practical, spiritual and emotional needs that these women can meet far better than men.

In closing, if we can learn anything for this work, let's learn to work together in spite of our differences of understanding. The local church is the body of Christ—let's minister with love, mercy and faithfulness!

Joseph R. Rogers, Sr.

Pastor/Teaches

VII. For Your Consideration:

I read an article by **Dan Blazer** as he discusses the role of **Phoebe** and women of the Church, that I found very interesting and it is my prayer that I will help brighten your understanding as it relates to whether or not *'women'* or *'female'* should be ordained into the office of **deacon(ness)**.

**Phoebe and the Role of Women as
Deaconesses in the Church
(Romans 16:1, 2, 7;
(I Timothy 3:11 - 13)**

"I commend to you our **sister Phoebe**, a servant of the church in Cenchrea. I ask you to receive her in the Lord in a way worthy of the saints and to give her any help she may need from you, for she has been a great help to many people, including me." (Romans 16:1, 2)

A Brief Historical Review:

Three groups of women during the post-New Testament period were thought to be recognized in special categories – the **virgins, widows** and **deaconesses.**

a. Virgins probably were not organized but consisted of younger women who dedicated themselves to **chastity, asceticism and service.** These women were considered of great value to the church. (I Timothy 3: 11 - 13)

    b. Widows were certainly organized and took on specific services (I Timothy 5:9, 10). **Deaconesses** most likely worked hand in hand with the male ministers, yet focused on working with females (given the social distance between men and women in society at that time).

    They frequently must have been the wives of deacons (and perhaps other church leaders) but it is not clear that this was a necessity.

    c. Deaconesses specifically assisted in the teaching and baptism of women. They generally did not teach the men.

Alexander Campbell believed that deaconesses were appointed in the New Testament church, yet he did not push their appointment during the early Restoration movement.

From Romans 16:1 as well as from I Timothy 3:11 it appears that females were constituted deaconesses in the primitive church. Duties to females, as well as to males, demand this." ("Order" *The Millennial Harbinger*, 1835)

Robert Milligan, a 19th century leader of the restoration movement, assumed the work of deaconesses did not extend to a teaching ministry. "The Diaconate of the primitive Church was not confined to male members. Deaconesses were also appointed to attend to the needs of the sick and the needy, especially of their own sex." ("**Of Deacons**", *The Millennial Harbinger*, **1855**)

Other supporters of deaconesses included **E.G. Sewell** (1893), **Hayden** (1894) who viewed deaconesses as wives of deacons. Restoration leaders who did not support the office of deaconess included **David Lipscomb, Gus Nichols, and Burton Coffman.**

In spite of the widely varying opinions regarding the appointment of deaconesses in the New Testament church, few churches in the Restoration movement have actually appointed deaconesses.

I. Romans 16:1, 2, 7

A. Phoebe.

1. These two short verses (16:1, 2) have been the center of the debate over whether women were appointed officially as deaconesses during New Testament times.

2. Phoebe is referred to as both **diakonos** and as a patroness or protectoress.

3. Many argue, including lexiconographers, that the term diakonos is used in the New Testament both in a general (e.g. Matthew 22:13) and the specific sense as a church official (I Timothy 3:8). The term used is the same and only the interpretation of the context assists in making this distinction.

4. In the secular world, the *diakonos* was used to describe various types of service, such as messengers, bakers and even statesmen.

5. On the one hand some would argue that Paul often uses *diakonos* in the general sense of servant or minister. (I Corinthians 3:5 and II Corinthians 3:6) He uses the term in a general sense in Romans 16:1.

a. These women could not be deacons in the special sense because one qualification of a deacon is that he is the husband of one wife and a woman clearly cannot be the husband of one wife.

b. These women clearly could have carried out many of the functions of deacons but this does not necessitate that they be formally recognized as deacons (hold an official office).

Their service would probably have been service to other women c. Not all parts of the body can be the head (that is, hold a position of spiritual leadership), yet they are equally valuable parts of the body. (I Corinthians 12:22)

    d. We should be more concerned with the work of a servant than the official role of a servant.

    e. Is Romans 16:1 the passage to which we should look for doctrinal guidance? Is it a theologically insignificant postscript? Is Paul is giving honor to whom honor is due and that's all? Was the women in Romans 16 fellow workers?

  6. On the other hand, some would argue that Paul appears to be using the term *diakonos* in the special sense in Romans 16:1.

 a. She is specifically noted to be a *diakonos* of the church in Cenchrea (unlike Paul's use of the term *diakonos* in referring to Tychikos [a dear brother and faithful servant] in Ephesians 6:21). In addition, if she had simply been singled out for her service, she probably would have been considered one of the "sisters", such as Mary in 16:6.

 b. Phoebe was a leader of the church at Cenchrea because of her status and labor for the entire church, not just her labor for women. Phoebe's actions were not gender specific.

c. It is not at all clear whether Phoebe (or male deacons for that matter) were officially appointed or simply recognized by this special designation if they fulfilled a special service (unlike the specific appointment of elders). The term *diakonos* is not used in Acts 6. (See below.)

d. The use of *diakonos* in Romans 16:1 cannot be distinguished from its use in Philippians 1:1.

e. The work of the deaconess was not limited to women. (Actually, if one accepts that women were appointed in the New Testament church as deaconesses, there is no direct evidence in scripture regarding whether their work was limited to women or not.)

7. Phoebe is also described as a *prostatis* (protectoress or patroness). Romans 16:1 is the only time this word is used in the New Testament in the feminine form. The use of the word is of only indirect significance to the question of whether women served as official deaconesses in the New Testament yet is important to consider.

a. The word in its various forms could mean both one who rules or leads (I Thessalonians 5:12) as well as one who cares for or gives aid to (Romans 12:8).

The evidence for the word in Romans 16:1 probably leans toward personal care in this passage rather than a governing officer.

    b. She probably was a woman of wealth and some influence.

    c. She may have been a widow (her husband is not mentioned) and therefore was a property owner and patron of the church in Cenchrea.

    d. She had served Paul (possibly supporting him financially).

    e. Her role as a patron (rather than manager) parallels her work as a servant and possible role as a deaconess.

    B. Junia (Junias), an interlude.

a. Almost all commentators agree that "Junias" in Romans 16:7 was a female and the proper translation is Junia. She very well may have been a relative of Andronicus (wife or sister). Early Christian writers unanimously took the name to be feminine (e.g. Origen).

b. The passage could read that Junia was an apostle or was recognized as outstanding by the apostles.

c. The term "apostle" or apostolos could mean one who had directly been sent by Christ (such as the twelve and Paul) or others specifically sent out as evangelists (Barnabas in Acts 14:14). It is clearly in the latter sense that Junia is being recognized.

4. The best rendering is probably that Junia was a fellow evangelist (a messenger of the word) with Paul. She suffered with Paul in the role of evangelist. Just as Priscilla and Aquila, Andronicus and Junia worked as a team. (During New Testament times it probably would have been extremely difficult for a woman to move about alone as an evangelist though she may well have served in this role near her home.

II. <u>I Timothy 3:11 - 13.</u>

A. Did Paul provide special instructions for women as deacons? If so, they are found in I Timothy 3:11 - 13.

B. The Greek term (derived from *gyne* and translated wife or woman) probably refers to either wives of deacons or deaconesses themselves. (A less likely interpretation is that the passage refers to women in general.)

C. On the view that Paul is referring to the wives of deacons:

1. The argument is made that Paul would not
sandwich qualifications for deaconesses (3:11) between the qualifications for deacons (3:8 - 10 and 3:12. 13).

2. In addition, why didn't Paul simply use the term *diakonos* to refer to the women?

D. On the view that Paul is referring to deaconesses:

1. The argument is made that Paul would not have given qualifications for the wives of deacons but not for the wives of bishops (elders).

2. The term *diakonos,* used in 3:8, covers the entire passage (3:8 – 3:13).

3. Verses 3:12, 13 may have been an "afterthought"

thus explaining the structure of the passage.

E. That the office of deacon (as opposed to simply being recognized as a servant) was recognized is clear from this passage (3:10). Nevertheless, it is uncertain whether there was a formal appointment (ordination) of deacons or whether deacons (and deaconesses) served well and after a time gain the recognition by the church (3:13).

If the latter is true, then the distinction between male and female deacons is much less clear (neither serve in a position of authority) and the possibility of female deacons (deaconesses) becomes more likely.

VIII. The Author's Contact And Other Works Information

1. **Mailing Address:**
    1313 Ujamaa Drive, Raleigh, NC 27610

2. Phone Nos.
    (919) 208-0200,

3. **Email Address:**
    jroger3420@aol.com,

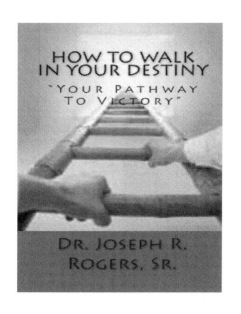

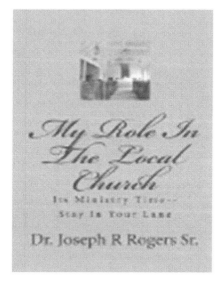

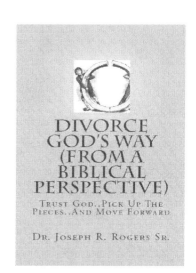

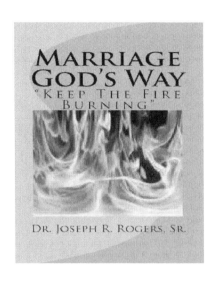

(There Is A Series of 1-39)

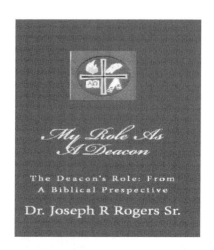

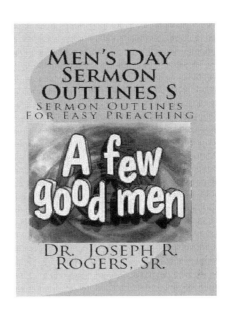

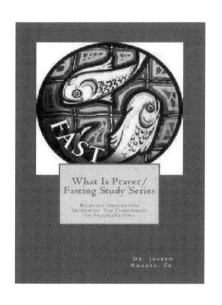

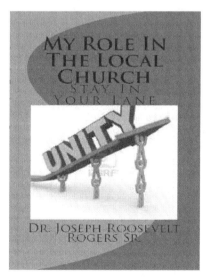

IX. Notes:

Made in the USA
Columbia, SC
26 September 2023